Table of Four

Angela Dianne Bell

Foreword

    In a world full of life's challenges and so many things that are clamoring for our attention, none are more important than family. I found food, specifically a good home cooked meal, to be the secret to getting my family together. Through good times and bad, those times of comfort, laughter and fun have become the memories that bind us together and keep us strong. This book is more than just a collection of good recipes or tasty meals. Think of it as an addition to your family's scrapbook of memories. Whether you're looking for some inspiration in the kitchen or a reason to get the family together, look no further than Table of four.

                                        Love Always,
                                        Blove

Copyright © 2021 Angela Dianne Bell

All rights reserved. No part of this publication may be reproduced, distributed, or transmitted in any form or by any means, including photocopying, recording, or other electronic or mechanical methods, without the prior written permission of the publisher, except in the case of brief quotations embodied in critical reviews and certain other noncommercial uses permitted by copyright law. For permission requests, write to the publisher at the address below.

Liberation's Publishing
183 Cottrell St.
West Point, MS. 39773
www.liberationspublishing.com

ISBN: 978-1-951300-78-4

Dedication

To Gary, Claudia, and Mikayla
Thank you all for making me the woman I am today, I hope I continue to make y'all proud. Love, mama.
To my honey, Michael
Thank you for loving me, I'm so grateful our hearts found each other again.

TABLE OF CONTENTS

Salads 13

    Bacon Spinach Salad 15

    Cole Slaw 17

    Cool Ranch Salad 19

    Corn Salad 21

    The Cup Salad 23

    Egg Salad Croissant 25

    English Pea Salad 27

    Fried Chicken Salad 29

    Grilled Chicken Caesar Salad 31

    Mediterranean Salad 33

    Potato Salad 35

    Rainbow Pasta Salad 37

    Seven Layer Salad 39

    Spaghetti Salad 41

    Wedge Salad 43

Main Dishes ... 45

Barbecued Salmon ... 47
Chicken and Dumplings ... 49
Chicken Parmesan Casserole ... 51
Chicken Salad Sandwich ... 53
Chilli ... 55
Country Catfish Tenders ... 57
Jerk Chicken Skewers ... 59
Lobster Tail Scampi ... 61
Macaroni and Cheese Stuffed Chicken ... 63
Philly Cheese Steak Sandwich ... 65
Pot Roast ... 67
Real Loaded Baked Potato ... 69
Salmon Croquettes ... 71
Shrimp and Grits ... 73
Southern Oxtails ... 75
Tuna Salad Sub ... 77

Side Dishes 79

    Cabbage Soup 81

    Cilantro Lime Rice 83

    The Best Friend Cornbread 85

    Easy Macaroni and Cheese 87

    Smoked Turkey Collard Greens 89

Desserts 91

    Peach Cobbler 93

    Strawberry Shortcake 95

    Whipping Cream Pound Cake 97

Entertaining 99

    Chef Salad Tray 101

    Grazing Tray 103

    Green Smoothie 105

    Guacamole 107

    Infused Water 109

    My Mama's Biscuits 111

Whipped Coffee 113

Salads

Bacon Spinach Salad

Prep Time 15 Minutes   Servings 4

Ingredient

- 8 slices of thick cut bacon
- 1 bag baby spinach
- 1 small red onion (diced)
- 1 package of mushrooms (sliced)
- 1 large tomato (diced)
- 1 large cucumber (sliced)
- 1/2 cup of blue cheese crumbles

Fry bacon until crispy, drained. Add Spinach to a serving platter. Top with bacon, cucumber, mushrooms, onions, tomatoes, and blue cheese crumbles. Serve with blue cheese dressing or desired dressing.

The bacon and spinach salad kind of reminds me of the wedge salad because of the combination of bacon and blue cheese. However, the veggies put a different spin on this salad which makes it delicious. I know many people are not fans of blue cheese dressing or crumbling, so you can substitute with feta cheese and the desired dressing.

Cole Slaw

Prep Time 30 Minutes   Servings 8

Ingredients

- 14oz bag of coleslaw mix
- 1 small red onion, diced.
- 1/2 cup of mayonnaise
- 1 lemon

- 1 tablespoon sugar
- 1 teaspoon apple cider vinegar
- 1 tablespoon peppercorn, grind

In a small mix of mayonnaise, lemon juice, sugar vinegar and peppercorn. Set dressing aside for 15 minutes. In a large bowl mix slaw, onions, and dressing.

I really have to have a taste for coleslaw and when I do I like to make it myself. Every restaurant's coleslaw is so different, and there is always a debate about which is the best. So, I decided to stop the debate and make my own.

Cool Ranch Salad

Prep Time 20 Minutes   Servings 4

Ingredients

- 1lb ground beef or turkey
- 1 large bag of Cool Ranch Doritos
- 1 packet taco seasoning
- 1 7oz can of corn nibblets
- 1 bag of shredded lettuce
- 1 bag of shredded sharp cheddar cheese
- 1 bag of shredded sharp cheddar cheese
- 1 large, chopped tomato.
- 1 cup of sour cream
- Small jar of salsa
- 1/2 of jalapenos

Brown ground meat, and drain. Add corn, seasoning and water according to packet. Mix well over low heat and simmer for 10 minutes. On a large serving tray layer Doritos, meat mixture, lettuce, tomatoes, cheese, salsa, jalapenos, and sour cream. Serve immediately.

Now there is a trend that is on the internet which is, "Taco Tuesday". Before eating tacos on a certain day, I was eating taco salad every day of the week. While many like taco salad with regular tortilla chips or cheese Doritos, I like Cool Ranch. I promise if you try them on this salad, you won't go back. LOL

Corn Salad

Prep Time 15 Minutes   Servings 4

Ingredients

- 1 can corn.
- 2 limes
- 5 oz grape tomatoes (quartered)
- 1/4 oz cilantro
- 1/2 purple onion (diced)
- 1/2 teaspoon sea salt

In a glass bowl pour in corn, and squeeze juice from both limes. Mix in quartered tomatoes, cilantro, onions, and salt. Refrigerate for an hour.

I don't like the corn salad that I grew up with, it has a mayo base. This corn salad is delicious to me, and it is fresh and easy to make. It can be served as a side dish, a salad or even a topping. My husband loves me to make his Pico de Gallo, so he is a fan of this salad, he said all he's missing is a taco. LoL

The Cup Salad

Prep Time 30 Minutes   Serving 4

Ingredients

- 1 head of iceberg lettuce (shredded)
- 1 cup of diced tomatoes
- 1 cup of diced cucumbers
- 1 cup of diced boiled eggs (4)
- 1 cup of diced green onions
- 1 cup of shredded cheddar cheese
- 1 cup of shredded parmesan cheese
- 1 cup of diced strawberries
- 1 cup of 2 diced chicken breasts (season as desired)

Season 2 chicken breast and cook until done. Boil eggs for 10 minutes. Put iceberg lettuce in a large serving bowl. Top all ingredients.

I wasn't sure what to name this salad, but as I began to write down the ingredients CUP was in all of them. So that's how The Cup Salad was born, I often tend to make up salads, so I guess this is one that I just made up. I hope you try it with your favorite dressings.

Egg Salad Croissant

Prep Time 20 Minutes   Servings 2

Ingredients

- 4 boiled eggs and chopped.
- 1/4 cup of mayonnaise
- 1 tablespoon mustard
- 1 tablespoon green onion, chopped.
- 1/2 teaspoon salt
- 1/2 teaspoon black pepper

Boil eggs for 10 minutes. Cover the eggs and remove them from heat for about 5 minutes. In a small bowl, add chopped eggs, mayo, mustard, onions, salt, and pepper.

I guess you have to be a fan of all things boiled eggs to appreciate the egg salad. Listen, you do not have a clue what you are missing as I was trying to find different recipes for this book. You know, the things that I have tried I stumble across this egg salad, and let's just say it will be on my breakfast table from here on out.

English Pea Salad

Prep Time 20 Minutes   Serving 4

Ingredients

- 2 Cans of young sweet peas
- large, boiled eggs, chopped.
- ½ cup of mayonnaise
- Pinch of salt
- Pinch of black pepper
- Tablespoon of sweet relish
- ½ small red onion, sliced thinly
- ½ cup of sharp cheddar cheese

Boil eggs for 10 minutes. Drain water off sweet peas. In a mixing bowl with peas, gently fold in eggs, mayonnaise, relish, onions and salt and pepper to taste. Top with shredded cheese. Refrigerate as desired and serve.

I always found English Peas to be kind of boring may it's just me. I know you can get them with carrots, but it still was boring to me. When I found out about the English Pea salad it was a GO, this salad is so good. I would suggest that you try it with fried chicken.

Fried Chicken Salad

Prep Time 25 Minutes   Servings 4

Ingredients

- 8 boneless, skinless chicken tenders
- 2 cups of all-purpose flour
- 2 teaspoons of salt
- 2 teaspoon pepper
- 1 tablespoon hot sauce
- 1 cup canola oil
- 1 package spring mix
- 4 Roma tomatoes (sliced)
- 1 cucumber (sliced)
- 1 bell pepper (diced)

Place tenders in a bowl with salt, pepper, hot sauce and toss. Top with flour and toss chicken. Heat a cup of oil until hot, add chicken. Fry on each side for 4 minutes until golden brown, drain on paper towel. Divide on 4 plates, spring mix, tomatoes, cucumber, bell pepper and top with 2 tenders each. Served with ranch dressing or desired dressing.

Fried chicken salad is also my favorite. I just love the fried chicken mix with the vegetables and the ranch dressing. The fried chicken also makes it very filling as well, so it can be eaten as a lunch or a dinner. Happy Eating!

Grilled Chicken Caesar Salad

Prep Time 20 Minutes   Serving 4

Ingredients

- 4 Boneless chicken breasts (cut into chunks)
- 4 Heads of Romaine Hearts
- Bag of Texas Toast croutons
- 1/4 cup of olive oil
- Tablespoon of minced garlic
- 1/2 teaspoon of salt
- 1/2 teaspoon of pepper
- Teaspoon of lemon pepper
- 16oz Bottle of Caesar dressing

In mixing bowl, whisk together oil, garlic, salt, pepper, and lemon pepper. Add chicken chunks. Marinate in refrigerator, covered for about 30 minutes. Cook chicken for about 10 minutes or until the internal temperature of 165°. Chop romaine hearts into bite size pieces. Put each heart on plates, top with chicken, cheese, and croutons. Drizzle each salad with dressings.

When I first learned about this salad it was very boring for me. Let's be clear the Caesar salad only has four ingredients, which are lettuce, cheese, crouton, and its Caesar dressing. I love salads that have over ten ingredients or more. It is actually good, but I needed some protein in it, hence the grilled chicken... Enjoy!

Mediterranean Salad

Prep Time 15 Minutes   Serving 2

Ingredient

Salad
- 10 ounces of mixed salad greens
- 1 can black olives and green olives rinsed and drained.
- Half of small red onion peeled and thinly sliced.
- Half of English cucumber thinly sliced.
- 1/2 cup diced roasted red peppers.
- 1/2 cup crumbled feta cheese

Dressing
- 1/3 cup of olive oil
- 2 tablespoons of red wine vinegar
- 2 teaspoon Dijon mustard
- 2 teaspoon dried oregano
- 1 teaspoon sea salt
- 1/2 teaspoon cracked black pepper.
- 1 teaspoon minced garlic

Mix all ingredients for Greek Vinaigrette dressing, set aside. Mix all ingredients for the salad, top with dressing.

I learned about this recipe from a lady that I affectionately called Mama Chef. She is one of the biggest supporters of my ministry and the ministry that I am a part of is Divine Connectors. This salad is so easy to make and delicious. It is called arugula, but the salad spring mix will do just fine.

Potato Salad

Prep Side 30 Minutes   Serving 8

Ingredients

- 6 potatoes (peeled) (chopped in cubes)
- 4 eggs
- 1/2 cup of mayo
- 2 tablespoons of mustard
- 2 tablespoons of sweet relish
- 1 small onion
- 1 teaspoon salt
- 1 teaspoon pepper
- 1/2 teaspoon paprika

Boil potatoes until tender but firm. Put eggs in water and bring them to a boil. Cover eggs and remove from heat. Let eggs remain in pan for about 5 minutes. In a mixing bowl, add potatoes eggs, onions, relish, mustard, mayonnaise, salt, and pepper. Garnish with paprika.

Potato salad is a must have at most family gatherings. With this salad, I know the instructions suggest refrigerating but I actually like mine warmth. It tastes so much better to me when it is first made, and everything is warm, try it.

Rainbow Pasta Salad

Prep Time 20 Minutes   Servings 8

Ingredients

- 1 bag tri-color rotini
- 1 can Rotel tomatoes (drained)
- 1 cucumber (sliced)
- 1 can of whole black olives (drained)
- 1 green onion stalk (sliced)
- 1 bottle Italian dressing
- 1 tablespoon olive oil
- 2 teaspoon salt (divided)
- 1 teaspoon pepper
- 1 teaspoon dry dill
- 1 teaspoon dry cilantro
- 1 teaspoon dry thyme
- 1 teaspoon brown sugar

Boil pasta with 1 teaspoon salt and oil for about 10 minutes or according to bag instructions. Drain and rinse with cool water. Mix tomatoes, cucumber, olives, and onions. Add a bottle of dressing, mix well. Add dry seasoning, mix well. Chill and serve.

I know I have another pasta salad in here too, but this is a good one. I think the color pasta and the vegetables are a beautiful combination for the mouth and eyes. Please don't make me choose which one is my favorite because I just couldn't, they're both delicious.

Seven Layer Salad

Prep Time 30 Minutes   Servings

Ingredients

- 1 head iceberg lettuce, chopped.
- 10oz grape tomatoes, halved.
- 1 package of shredded cheese
- 1 can sweet peas, drained.
- 1 12oz package bacon

- 1 cup of mayonnaise
- 2 tablespoons sugar
- 1 small bag of radishes, sliced

Cook bacon according to package or until crispy. Mix mayonnaise and sugar, refrigerate until ready to use. In a large glass bowl begin layer as follows: Lettuce, Tomatoes, Peas, Cheese, Radish, Dressing, Bacon

This is one of those salads that are just too pretty to eat, you just want to look at the presentation. The 7 layered salad is a salad for entertaining or trying to impress like you know how to cook.

Spaghetti Salad

Prep Time 20 Minutes   Serving 8

Ingredients

- 1 pound Spaghetti noodles
- 1 cup Cherry Tomatoes
- 4 small Cucumber, chopped.
- 1 cup Spinach
- 1 cup diced Ham
- 1 cup parmesan cheese
- 1 tablespoon Salad Supreme seasoning
- 1 15oz bottle Italian dressing

In boiling pot, cook spaghetti for 10-12 minutes until Al Dente', drain and rinse spaghetti in a mixing bowl. Add tomatoes, cucumbers, ham 1/2 cup cheese and salad supreme. Pour all dressing and mix well. Top with remaining cheese. Chill as desired.

> This dish is very near and dear to my heart. I was introduced to spaghetti salad by my sister Demetrice. This was her signature dish to bring to our gatherings. Demetrice passed away January 12,2015. I really don't make spaghetti salad that much anymore and that is why I changed some ingredients in the salad. I miss her every day, and some may not understand that certain foods can be a trigger. I hope you try this recipe with some fried chicken or catfish, which is how we would eat it.
> Continue to rest, sweet sister.

Wedge Salad

Prep Time 30 Minutes Servings 4

Ingredients

- 1 head of iceberg lettuce
- 1 package cherry tomatoes (diced)
- 8 slices of bacon
- 1 cup crumbled blue cheese.
- ½ cup chopped scallions
- Bottle of Blue Cheese dressing

Preheat oven to 350°. Cook bacon for 20 minutes or until it is crisp to crumble. Wash the lettuce head into 4 wedges. Begin building the salad by placing 1 wedge on each of 4 plates. Drizzle blue cheese dressing over each wedge. Scatter crumbled bacon, diced tomatoes, crumbled blue cheese and scallions over each salad.

I found out about the wedge salad on a lunch date with one of my sisters. I am not sure which one so I'm not going to say a name. Lol. I do remember that it was at a restaurant called Fair Park Grill and we thought we were very fancy.

Main Dishes

Barbecued Salmon

Prep Time 4 Hours 15 Minutes   Servings 2

Ingredients

- 2 Salmon Filets
- 1/2 cup Barbecue Sauce
- 1 tablespoon lemon juice
- 1/2 lemon
- 1 tablespoon soy sauce
- 1 garlic clove (minced)
- 1 tablespoon liquid smoke
- 1 teaspoon ground black pepper
- 1 teaspoon brown sugar
- 1 tablespoon olive oil

In a mixing bowl, mix 1/4 cup of barbecue sauce, lemon juice, soy sauce, garlic, liquid smoke, black pepper, and brown sugar to make a marinate. Refrigerating for at least four hours overnight would be perfect. On the top stove, heat, a griddle pans with olive oil, cook to your desired temperature for doneness, brush with remaining barbecue sauce, squeeze lemon over the filet and serve.

I just recently discovered that salmon can be eaten medium or medium rare, just like a steak, did you know that? My cooking time for salmon is normally 7 minutes on each side but if you prefer less then go at it. I have to cook salmon just for myself because my husband doesn't like it, I know you don't know what he is missing.

Chicken and Dumplings

Prep Time 2 Hours   Servings 8

Ingredients

- 8 chicken leg quarters
- 2 cups of flour
- 1 tablespoon salt
- 1 tablespoon black pepper
- 1 tablespoon garlic powder
- 1 tablespoon onion powder
- 1 tablespoon seasoning salt
- 1 tablespoon of Goya Adobo all-purpose seasoning
- 1 teaspoon red pepper flakes

In a large stock pot fill with water. Add chicken and all seasonings Cook on medium high for 60 minutes. In a mixing bowl add flour. Add chicken broth from pot as needed to make dumpling soft and firm but not sticky. On a floured surface, knead dough with a rolling pin. Cut into inch squares. Stir into stock pot and cook for 30 minutes.

Chicken and dumplings are one of those filing one pot meals that go a long way. This recipe is a favorite of my children as well. When I make this, I can expect knocks at the door, with bowls in their hands.

Chicken Parmesan Casserole

Prep Time 2 Hours   Servings 8

Ingredients

- 1 whole chicken
- 3 cups of penne pasta
- 1 package of whole mushrooms, diced.
- 1 small onion, diced.
- 1 bell pepper, diced.
- 2 cans 24oz of spaghetti sauce
- 1 can rotel tomatoes
- 1 teaspoon salt
- 1 teaspoon pepper
- 1 tablespoon Italian spices
- 5oz shaved parmesan cheese.
- 1 package slice mozzarella

In a large pot boil chicken with salt, pepper, and Italian spices until failing from bone. Remove chicken, pour in pasta in chicken broth. Cook pasta according to directions. In a saucepan, sauteed mushrooms, onions, bell peppers and Rotel tomatoes. Pour in spaghetti sauce and 3oz parmesan cheese In a large casserole dish mix chicken and pasta. Pour in sauce mixture. Layer slice mozzarella cheese. Bake for 30 minutes. Top with remaining parmesan cheese. Bake for 10 minutes. Garnish with basil.

I was having some people over and was thinking about what to serve and this recipe came to mind. I know chicken parmesan is normally with fried chicken, but I didn't want to do that. I wanted to make a big enough pan for seconds. So, if you want a one dish meal that will feed guests try this one with biscuits, they will be good and full.

Chicken Salad Sandwich

Prep Time 20 Minutes   Servings 8

Ingredients

- 1 store bought rotisserie chicken (3lbs)
- 1 1/2 cup mayonnaise
- 1 cup green grapes, halves and seedless
- 1/2 cup sweet relish
- 4 boiled eggs, chopped.
- 1 teaspoon salt
- 1 teaspoon pepper

Hand shred chicken. Mix in bowl with mayonnaise, grapes, and relish eggs. Season with salt and pepper. Cover and refrigerate until chilled. Serve with lettuce and tomatoes. Make a sandwich.

I know many people like to eat this salad with crackers or even on a vegetable tray. I love chicken salad on bread with the trimmings of lettuce and tomatoes. If I am feeling really bold, I will throw some pickles in the mix. It is very delicious for a lunch or dinner; I haven't tried it at breakfast yet but that doesn't mean you can't. Enjoy!

Chilli

Prep Time 1 Hour   Servings 8

Ingredients

- 1/2 cup scallions (diced)
- 1 bell pepper (diced)
- 2 tablespoons of chili powder
- 1 teaspoon dried oregano
- 1 teaspoon garlic powder
- 1 teaspoon ground cumin
- 1/2 teaspoon salt
- 1 tablespoon sugar
- 1 tablespoon flour
- 1 Pound ground beef
- 7 oz Hill shire sausage
- 1 can diced tomatoes.
- 1 can kidneys beans
- 1 can pinto beans
- 1 can of black beans
- 1 cup beer
- 2 cups of water (divided)

In a saucepan, cook beef, scallions and bell pepper, over medium heat 10 minutes, stir occasionally Mix flour and 1 cup water, put aside Drain beef mixture in a strainer. In a large pot put beef mixture, chili powder, oregano, cumin, salt, sugar, tomatoes, water, and beer. Bring mixture to a boil Stir in beans with the liquids, and flour mixture, bring to a boil. Reduce heat, cook uncovered for 30 minutes, stir occasionally until desired thickness. Top with cheese, sour cream, or desired topping.

Listen, my chili is by far my children's favorite meal to eat from me. I must cook enough for them to eat after I cook it, and enough for all three of them to take a carry out bowl. I bought Fritos scoops, shredded cheddar cheese and sour cream to bring it all together, and they love it. So, this is for my three smart and beautiful children.

Country Catfish Tenders

Prep Time 20 Minutes   Servings 4

Ingredients

- 4 catfish fillets, cut into strips.
- 2 cups of seasoned fish breading mix
- 2 tablespoons Cajun seasoning
- 1 quart canola oil

In large pot or deep fryer heat oil to 365°. In gallon Ziploc bag mix breading, Cajun seasoning, and fish. Shake excess breading off and drop in oil. Cook for about 5 minutes until golden brown or normally fish floats to top.

I could not do a cookbook without putting my family's favorite thing in it, fish. Listen, we normally eat fish at every gathering whether it's catfish or freshwater fish such as bream. When I tell you fish is a thing in our family, and even more we love the sport of fishing. As I am writing this, I sense a fish fry on the way.

Jerk Chicken Skewers

Prep Time 60 Minutes   Servings 4

Ingredients

- 1 pound chicken breasts, cut into chunks.
- 1 cup of rice
- 1 teaspoon grated lime rind
- 2 tablespoon cilantros
- 1/2 teaspoon salt
- lime halves, to serve

- 1 small onion, quartered.
- 1 tablespoon minced garlic
- 1 tablespoon chopped ginger.
- 1 tablespoon ground allspice
- 1/2 lime juice
- 2 tablespoons of olive oil

Soak 8 wooden skewers in water for 30 minutes. In a blender or food processor put in all jerk sauce ingredients. Transfer to a bowl and mix in chicken chunks. Cover and let stand for 5 minutes. Cook rice as instructed, drained, and stir in lime rind, cilantro, and lime juice. Thread the chicken onto skewers and cook for about 15 minutes, turning often. Plate serving dish with rice, and place chicken skewers on top. Add lime halves.

You know how you get tired of cooking the same thing, well this is where this recipe came from. I have many cookbooks so I can get inspiration and ideas for meals. The Jerk Chicken is delicious, I added and subtracted some things, and you can do the same.

Lobster Tail Scampi

Prep Time 45 Minutes   Servings 4

Ingredients

- 8 lobster tails
- 1 pound angel hair pasta
- 1/4 cup parmesan cheese
- 1 stick salted butter
- 2 tablespoons of minced garlic
- 1/4 cup lemon juice
- 1/4 cup fresh cilantro
- 2 tablespoons Cajun seasoning
- 1 tablespoon olive oil

Melt butter in saucepan, stir in garlic, lemon juice, cilantro, and Cajun seasoning, set aside. Preheat oven to 400°. Pace lobster on a baking sheet, top with some butter mixture, cook about 20 minutes. Cook angel hair pasta, al dente'. Mix butter mixture, parmesan cheese and pasta and plate. Top with two lobster tails.

I first tasted scampi sauce at the infamous Red Lobster restaurant. I have now learned how to make scampi sauce at home, and you can add anything to it, shrimp, chicken or even lobster tails. It is a fancy dish, I might try this for a date night with, The Honey.

Macaroni and Cheese Stuffed Chicken

Prep Time 1 Hour 30 Minutes   Servings 4

Ingredients

- whole chicken
- 1 teaspoon salt
- 1 teaspoon pepper
- 1 teaspoon garlic powder
- 1 teaspoon paprika
- 1 teaspoon dry basil
- 1 teaspoon ground sage
- 1 teaspoon dry rosemary
- 1 teaspoon thyme
- 1 teaspoon red pepper flakes
- 1 tablespoon olive oil

Preheat oven to 400°. Mix all seasonings together, set aside. Dry chicken with paper towels and rubbed down with olive oil. Rub seasoning all over chicken Roast chicken for 30 minutes. Cook macaroni as desired, or recipe is in this book. Turn oven down to 350° for another 30 minutes. Pull chicken out of the oven, cut down the middle and begin to stuff with macaroni. Turn the oven off, and let the dish set in for 10 minutes.

I saw this dish on YouTube, and I was like, wow that looks delicious. The Youtuber was eating it, and I think she said she found it on Instagram, so I decided to make my own version. I think I just like the presentation of it because it is a whole meal in one.

Philly Cheese Steak Sandwich

Prep Time 30 Minutes   Servings 4

Ingredients

- 1 1/2 lb. thinly sliced ribeye steak
- 1 medium onion thinly sliced.
- 1 bell pepper thinly sliced.
- 8 slices of Swiss cheese
- 4 Hoagie bun
- 1 teaspoon salt
- 1 teaspoon pepper
- 1 teaspoon garlic powder
- 4 tablespoon mayo
- 2 tablespoons of olive oil

Over medium heat adds oil, onion, and bell peppers. Sauteed vegetables about 5 minutes, remove and put aside. In the same pan add steak, cook until tender or desired. Add vegetables, salt, pepper, garlic powder and simmer for about 5 minutes. Divide meat mixture into four, cover each portion with two slices of cheese. Toast buns if desired and scoop mixture onto buns.

I think the only person that I know personally doesn't like Philly cheesesteak is my youngest daughter, Mikayla. She just is not a fan, I don't know if it's the meat or vegetables or just the combination of everything. However, she and I are not a fan of cheese on our burger so that might be the hesitation of it all. Lol

Pot Roast

Prep Time 3 Hours   Servings 8

Ingredients

- 3-pound chuck roast
- 2 tablespoons of olive oil
- 1 tablespoon sea salt
- 1/4 teaspoon fresh ground black pepper
- 1 medium yellow onion
- 1 bell pepper
- 14 ounce can of carrots
- 1 bay leaf
- 1 garlic clove, minced.
- 7 medium potatoes peeled only.
- 1 tablespoon of flour

Rub 1 tablespoon of olive oil onto the roast, sprinkle with salt and pepper. Sear meat on each side for about 5 minutes. Add bay leaf and garlic. Cover and bake for 1 hour. Drain meat broth from roast, put aside. Add onions, bell pepper, and carrots. Cover and bake for another 1 hour. In a saucepan, heat 1 tablespoon of olive oil. Add flour, cook until flour is brown. Add broth until it becomes gravy, pour gravy mixture over roast, bake for another 30 minutes, let stand for 10 minutes and serve.

Pot roast is one of my favorites "one pot" meals. It has meat, potatoes, and veggies all in one pot. It is to put the meal in the center of the table, and leave my perfect meal for Sunday dinner, so I decided to share with you the recipe. I always just family just "buffet" it with rice, biscuits, and molasses, those were the good ole days.

Real Loaded Baked Potato

Prep Time 1 Hour 30 Minutes   Servings 4

Ingredients

- 4 large baking potatoes
- 1 lb. sliced sirloin steak
- 1 lb. shrimp, deveined.
- 1 lb. Cajun sausage links, sliced.
- 2 cups Velveeta cheese, cubed
- 1 cup shredded pepper jack cheese
- 1 cup milk
- 1 can Rotel tomatoes
- 2 tablespoons of olive oil

Preheat oven to 400°. Wash potatoes and place them in oven for about an hour In large pot add milk, cheeses and can of tomatoes on low heat. In skillet add oil and steak, cook until tender. Add shrimp and sausage. Add meat mixture to cheese mixture. Plate potatoes and cut down middle, top with meat and cheese mixture.

My honey and I went on a date and had a fajita potato from a Mexican restaurant. It was delicious but we weren't too fond of all the onions and bell peppers, so I substituted those for more meat. My honey is a straight meat and potato man, so you can guess that this is one of his favorite dishes.

Salmon Croquettes

Prep Time 30 Minutes   Servings 4

Ingredients

- 1 can pick salmon.
- 2 tablespoons of flour
- 2 tablespoons of diced green onions, diced.
- 1 teaspoon seasoning salt
- 1 teaspoon black pepper
- 1 egg
- 1/4 cup canola oil

Drain and debone salmon. In a mixing bowl, stir in salmon, flour, onion, seasoning salt, egg, and black pepper. Mix well. Make four patties with mixture. Heat oil over medium high heat, fry patties until golden brown.

If you have never eaten a salmon croquette, you are missing out. I remember eating these at every home I went to as a little girl. My mama, grandmama and my aunties would all serve these.

Shrimp and Grits

Prep Time 30 Minutes   Servings 4

Ingredients

- 1 cup grits
- 1 lb. shrimp, deveined.
- 1/2 cup diced onions.
- 1/2 cup diced bell peppers.
- 1/2 cup sliced mushrooms.
- 1/2 cup water

- 2 tablespoons of butter, divided.
- 1 teaspoon salt of salt.
- 1 teaspoon black pepper, divided.
- 1 tablespoon flour

Cook grit according to package for about 15 minutes. Remove from heat stir in 1 tablespoon butter, 1/2 teaspoon salt and 1/2 teaspoon black pepper. In saucepan add butter and flour cook until brown, add water to make a creamy roux. Add onions, bell pepper, shrimp and remaining salt and pepper. Simmer for about 10 minutes.

In the last decade or so, shrimp and grits have become really popular, but it has been a "thing" for over 70 years. I have been to many brunches that shrimp and grits have been the star of the show. You can also add bacon to this recipe, just cook bacon and crumble it up on top of the shrimp. Enjoy!

Southern Oxtails

Prep Time 3 Hours, 30 Minutes

Ingredients

- 8 beef oxtails
- 1 cup flour, divided.
- 1 tablespoon salt
- 1 tablespoon pepper
- 1 tablespoon garlic powder
- 1 tablespoon seasoning salt
- 2 bouillon beef cubes
- 1/4 cup olive oil
- 4 cups of water

Preheat oven to 350°. Heat oil in large cast iron skillet. Season oxtails with salt, pepper, garlic powder, and seasoning salt. Coat the oxtails with the remaining flour. Brown oxtails in oil on each side in skillet, remove and place in large Dutch oven. Remove oil from skillet and keep the dripping. Whisk in flour slowly, add oil if needed. When flour is brown add water and beef bouillon cubes. Bring gravy to a boil and pour over oxtails. Place it in oven and cook for 3 hours.

Oxtails just soothe the spirit. I mean with the exception that they are expensive but comforting, nonetheless. They fall into the soul food category which means they are certainly good for the soul, Lol. You can put them on top of rice or alongside collard greens and cornbread, either way delicious.

Tuna Salad Sub

Prep Time 15 Minutes   Servings 4

Ingredients

- 2 12 oz cans of tuna
- 1/2 cup of mayonnaise
- 1/3 cup of mustard
- 1/3 cup of sweet relish
- 1 small onion (caramelized)
- Teaspoon salt
- Teaspoon salt
- Teaspoon black pepper
- 4 Hoagie rolls
- 2 medium tomatoes
- Lettuce leaves (optional)
- Pickles(optional)

Cook onion in skillet until caramelized. Combine drained tuna, onions, mayonnaise, mustard, relish, salt, and pepper. Assemble sandwiches on hoagie buns with lettuce, tomatoes, and pickles. Top with tuna salad.

There are several different ways the I like to eat tuna salad, but I think as a sandwich is my favorite. I eaten this salad with crackers and even on an actual salad with vegetables. I like the taste of tuna salad on a hoagie bun with the bread, it just takes it to another level. Enjoy!

Side Dishes

Cabbage Soup

Prep Time 45 Minutes   Servings 4

Ingredients

- 1 bag coleslaw mix (cabbage and carrots)
- 4 Roma tomatoes, halved.
- 2- 32oz vegetable broth
- 4 celery stalks thinly diced.
- 1 bell pepper, diced.
- 1 tablespoon garlic powder
- 1 teaspoon salt
- 1 teaspoon black pepper
- 1/2 teaspoon dried basil
- 1/2 teaspoon dried thyme
- 2 tablespoon paste

In a pot add oil, onions, celery, and bell pepper. Cook until vegetables are tender. Add broth, seasonings, and tomato paste. Cook for 5 minutes, Add cabbage and tomatoes. Simmer for 30 minutes.

I stumbled across this recipe trying to lose weight, and the first cabbage soup I found was not good. So, I decided to create my own because I love all things tomato based. This is a delicious soup.

Cilantro Lime Rice

Prep Time 20 minutes   Servings 4

Ingredients

- 2lb bag of collard greens
- 1 smoked turkey wing
- 1 tablespoon liquid smoke
- 1 tablespoon salt
- 1 tablespoon pepper
- 1 tablespoon brown sugar
- 1 tablespoon garlic powder
- 1 teaspoon red pepper flakes
- 1 small purple onion, diced.
- 1 tablespoon paprika
- 2 tablespoon apple cider vinegar

Rinse rice. In the pot add rice, water, salt, and tablespoon of butter. Bring to a boil for about 10 minutes. Remove from heat and cover, Add lime juice, 2 tablespoons cilantro and remaining butter. Garnish with lime peel and remaining cilantro.

Chipotle is another great restaurant of mine. The cilantro lime rice is the foundation of most of their dishes. So, I had to learn how to make it my way, and I must say that it is delicious.

The Best Friend Cornbread

Prep Time 45 Minutes   Servings 8

Ingredients

- 1 cup white cornmeal
- 1 cup of yellow cornmeal
- 1/2 cup self-rising flour
- 1/2 cup sugar
- 1 cup of buttermilk
- 1 egg
- 1 stick Land O' Lakes butter
- 1 teaspoon mayonnaise

Preheat oven to 350°. Grease rectangle baking pan. In a mixing bowl, mix cornmeal, flour sugar well. Stir in buttermilk, egg, mayonnaise, and melted butter. Pour in grease pan, bake for 20 to 25 minutes.

One of my best friend's cornbread is a must for a lot of my meals. I met her in 2015 and one of the best things about her is the cornbread. Lol. no, I'm kidding but it is delicious! I wanted to share her recipe because she has been just a gem in my life during some of my darkest moments. I hope you enjoy it as much as the people that love her do.

Easy Macaroni and Cheese

Prep Time 45 Minutes   Servings 4

Ingredients

- 2 cups of elbow macaroni
- 1/2 teaspoon salt
- 1/2 teaspoon black pepper
- 2 tablespoons of butter, divided.
- 1 cup milk
- 1 egg
- 1 cup shredded sharp cheddar.
- 1 cup shredded pepper jack
- 1 cup shredded Colby jack
- 1 cup shredded gouda

Cook macaroni according to package, adding salt and tablespoon of butter. In a large pot add milk, cheese, butter, and black pepper. Stir constantly until cheese is melted and mixture is creamy. In baking dish pour cool macaroni, butter, and beaten egg, stir. Pour cheese mixture over and stir. If desired, top with more cheese. In preheated oven, bake for 20 minutes.

We all know that macaroni and cheese is a must have in most American homes. You can't have a family dinner without this side dish. There are so many different ways to make macaroni and cheese but just try this easy recipe and let me know what you think.

Smoked Turkey Collard Greens

Prep Time 2 Hours 15 minutes   Servings 8

Ingredients

- 2lb bag of collard greens
- 1 smoked turkey wing
- 1 tablespoon liquid smoke
- 1 tablespoon salt
- 1 tablespoon pepper
- 1 tablespoon brown sugar
- 1 tablespoon garlic powder
- 1 teaspoon red pepper flakes
- 1 small purple onion, diced.
- 1 tablespoon paprika
- 2 tablespoon apple cider vinegar

Clean the collards in a sink with water and a tablespoon of vinegar. In a large pot with water, add turkey wings. Stir in salt, pepper, brown sugar, garlic powder, red pepper flakes, paprika and remaining vinegar. Cook for 30 minutes. Stir in collard greens. Cook for 1 hour and 30 minutes or until desired tenderness.

Collard greens are my favorite greens, I think... because I love all greens, but I really like collards. I believe I like them because my family does, we always try to see who can cook them the best because they are very hard to season if you don't know what you are doing. We can safely say that I am the "Collard Green Chef." Shhh. don't tell my family.

Desserts

Peach Cobbler

Prep Time 1 Hour   Servings 8

Ingredients

- 2- 15oz cans of sliced peaches
- 1 box of refrigerated pie crust (2 crusts)
- 1 tablespoon cinnamon
- 1 teaspoon nutmeg
- 1 tablespoon vanilla
- 1/2 cup of sugar
- 1 stick of butter
- 1 tablespoon of flour
- 1/2 cup of water (warmed)

Pour cans of peaches, cinnamon, nutmeg, sugar, vanilla, and butter in pan. Bring the mixture to a boil. Heat oven to 375. Mix flour with warm water and pour in mixture. Continue to let simmer. Cut first crust into small dumpling pieces into mixture. Pour into baking dish. Cover with the last crust and put it in oven for about 30 minutes or until crust is golden brown.

The peach cobbler is everyone's favorite, I think. However, there are some that do not like warm fruit, but cobblers are my friend. This recipe is very easy and tastes as if you had grown your own peaches and made your own dough. I serve it with whipped cream, but I am sure that ice cream will be even better.

Strawberry Shortcake

Prep Time 15 Minutes   Servings 4

Ingredients

- 2 cups of strawberries, sliced.
- 8 whole strawberries
- 2 tablespoons sugar
- 1 16oz cool whip
- 1 loaf of frozen pound cake, thawed

Mix sliced strawberries and sugar in bowl, set aside. Slice pound cake into 12 even slices. Place 3 slices on each plate. Cover with strawberry mixture. Top with cool whip. Place 2 strawberries on each plate for garnish.

Listen, strawberry shortcake was our go to dessert when I was a little girl. My mama would fix this for us almost every other week, her pound cake would be Sara Lee's. I thought it was the best thing; it is so necessary to hold some of those special little treats and desserts as a child close to your heart.

Whipping Cream Pound Cake

Prep Time 2 Hours   Servings 12

Ingredients

- 3 cups of cake flour
- 3 sticks of butter, softened.
- 6 eggs
- 3 cups of sugar
- 1\2-pint heavy whipping cream
- 3 tablespoons vanilla extract

Preheat oven to 350. Lightly flour and butter Bundt pan. In a mixing bowl, mix sugar and butter. Add eggs one at a time, mixing after each one. Alternatively add flour and whipping cream, blend. Stir in vanilla and pour in Bundt pan. Bake for 90 minutes or until a toothpick comes out clean. Cool completely and serve.

One of my friends introduced me to this cake and let me tell you it is delicious; it is an understatement. I made a mistake and added too much vanilla the second time I made this cake but realized I liked it better with more vanilla. It is a very rich cake, so all you will need is a glass of milk, a cup of coffee or even a glass of cold water.

Entertaining

Chef Salad Tray

Prep Time 30 Minutes   Servings 6

Ingredients

- Salad Mix
- Diced tomatoes.
- Diced ham.
- Purple onions
- Bacon bits
- Diced eggs.
- Diced cucumber.
- Shredded cheese

Boil eggs as desired. Dice eggs, cucumbers, onions, and tomatoes. Pace salad mixes in center and top with tomatoes. Place the remaining ingredients around salad mix.

I had a dinner party for my two sisters, their birthdays are just days apart. So instead of making individual salad bowls I started piling the salad on a tray. We had a great time that night, and I gifted them with cozy throw blankets because they are always cold. Lol

Grazing Tray

Prep Time 30 Minutes   Servings 4

Ingredients

- Peach Jam
- Zooberry Jam
- Dijon Mustard
- Jalapeno Cream Cheese
- Walnuts
- Green Grapes
- Raisins
- Honey Ham
- Smoke Sausage
- Cheddar Cheese
- Sliced Tomatoes
- Radish
- Saltine Crackers
- White Cheddar Crackers
- Olives
- Limes

Slice tomatoes, limes, sausage and ham, place as desired. Began designing tray as desired with remaining ingredients.

I just started using grazing boards, and they are great for entertaining. This is the perfect idea for serving food, your guests can just graze the board and go. Oh, a great conversation starter, too.

Green Smoothie

Prep Time

Ingredient

- 1 cup of Ice
- 1/2 cup of Orange Juice
- 1/2 Banana
- 1 Kiwi
- 1 cup of Spinach
- Limes

Mix all ingredients in a blender. Blend until smooth. Pour and Enjoy

We have approached a new year, so it is back to trying to be healthy again. My son bought me a smoothie blender a couple of Christmases ago, so back to green smoothies we go.

Guacamole

Prep Time 15 Minutes   Servings 2

Ingredients

- 1 medium Tomato, diced.
- 1 lime
- 1 small Onion, diced
- 1/4 cup Cilantro
- 2 Avocados, diced.
- Dash of salt and pepper

Mix tomato, onion, cilantro, and avocados well. Squeeze in lime juice. Season with salt and pepper to taste.

When you clean your refrigerator make sure you use the vegetables before they ruin. One of my favorites is avocado, so I made guacamole. Avocado has many health benefits and is low in calories. It is really good on toast as well, try it.

Infused Water

Prep Time 10 Minutes   Servings 8

Ingredients

- 1 cucumber, sliced.
- 1 granny apple, sliced.
- 1 red apple, sliced.
- 1 orange, sliced
- 1 lemon sliced.
- 1 lime, sliced.
- Gallon water

Slice all fruits and vegetables. Add all fruits and vegetables to water. Refrigerate overnight.

I've learned how to drink more water, so I started to add different fruits and vegetables to the water. For so long, I just didn't take the time to drink water, I would grab a soda or some type of juice. This infused recipe has helped me drink more; it can last in the refrigerator for about a week.

My Mama's Biscuits

Prep Time 25 Minutes   Servings 8

Ingredients

- 2 cups of Self-Rising Flour
- 1/2 Stick of Cold Butter
- 1 Tablespoon Shortening.
- 1/2 cup of Cold Buttermilk

Combine butter and Shortening into dry flour until thoroughly Incorporated. Pour in 1/2 cups of Cold Buttermilk. Mix gently until dough is firm. Flour board, transfer dough onto board. Knead for 5 minutes, keeping hands floured to prevent sticking. Roll dough out, using a biscuit cutter or round can, cut the desired number of biscuits. Place it in greased pan. Place it in oven for 12 minutes or until golden brown. Brush with butter. Serve with favorite dish.

My mama definitely cooks with love, she takes her time and cleans as she goes. A lot of your skills are deeply instilled in me and how I move in the kitchen. So, I had to put one of her recipes in this book, and what's better than some homemade buttermilk biscuits.

Whipped Coffee

Prep Time 5 Minutes   Servings 1

Ingredients

- 1 tablespoon instant coffee
- 1 tablespoon sugar
- 1 tablespoon hot water

Add coffee, sugar, and water with electric mixture until whipped and fluffy. Pour milk in glass over ice. Spoon mixture over milk.

This recipe was found during quarantine because so many people love coffee, I prefer iced coffee. The whipped coffee shown up on the internet, the proper name is, Dalgona coffee. It was delicious, when all the coffee houses were closed down my love for coffee found Dalgona.

www.ingramcontent.com/pod-product-compliance
Lightning Source LLC
Chambersburg PA
CBRC090910230426
43673CB00017B/421